Conversations with
Black Millionaire Entrepreneurs:
No Non-Sense Lessons from Those
Who've Been There, Done That!

By

Bro. Bedford, Founder
The Association Of Black Entrepreneurs

ASSOCIATION OF
BLACK ENTREPRENEURS

Conversations With Black Millionaire Entrepreneurs: No Non-Sense Lessons from Those Who've Been There, Done That!

By BROTHER BEDFORD
© Copyright 2014 Global Marketing & Publishing LLC.
All Rights Reserved.

DISCLAIMER AND/OR LEGAL NOTICES:

Cover Design and layout by Anthony Stewart ~ www.anthonystewart.net

Also by Bro. Bedford:

How to Be a Black Entrepreneur in the Age of Connectivity

The series- Conversations with Black Millionaire Entrepreneurs: No-Nonsense Lessons from Those Who've Been There, Done That!

Meet Bro. Bedford online and receive free training at:

www.brobedford.com

This Book is dedicated to all those who have a sincere desire to be entrepreneurs, to bring out the best of what God has placed in you. It is my earnest Prayer that this book helps you
on your journey.

<u>GIVING THANKS</u>

I'd like to give thanks to the God, the Author and Creator of the Heavens and Earth.

I'd like to give thanks to my family for all of the support and love that they have given me over the years.

I'd like to give a special thanks to My Wonderful, Loving, and Supportive Wife and our beautiful children.

I'd like to give thanks and deep appreciation to Cathy Hughes, Les Brown, George Fraser, Dennis Kimbro, Randal Pinkett, Lisa Nichols, Andrew Morrison and many more for allowing me into their world to share the message of Black Entrepreneurship to our people. I've learned so much thank you.

I'd also like to thank all of those who subscribe to my newsletters, lists, and buy my products. I Hope and Pray that this Book and my other courses are beneficial to you.

To Your Victory and Success,

Bro. Bedford

<u>Contents of this Book</u>

My Conversation with Les Brown

Effective Speaking…Developing your Mindset…Having a smarter group…Communication skills…the secret to a $640,000 contract…the power of small numbers…Mental Conditioning

My Conversation with Cathy Hughes

The start of a Media Empire…Overcoming sexism… The importance of a Banking Relationship…The Quiet Storm…Talk Radio…First Steps for Black Women…Most Important trait for Business

Preface

There will never be a shortage of someone giving you advice on what you should be doing in your business and personal life. The question becomes are they qualified to give the advice they are giving. The bigger question is why you are allowing unqualified individuals to give you advice on how to shape and guide your future.

My life is all about shortcuts. No that doesn't mean that I look for the easy way to do things, however that is not a bad thing either. But it does mean that I strive very hard to equip myself with the knowledge necessary to accomplish the task at hand. And that means seeking out qualified individuals and gaining the education and experience that they have to offer that adds value to my life.

And I don't mind paying for it, no matter what the cost. If I could pay $1,000 and receive a technique, receive insight that could add $10,000 worth of value to my life why wouldn't I. It's a no brainer for me.

This Book just scratches the surface on such a broad subject as Black Entrepreneurship. You have well over $2 billion worth of business experience coming from those that I interviewed. We would not have enough space to answer every question in a 100 books, but in this series we do answer some.

My life has been enriched by interviewing these giants of ours and I Hope and Pray your life will become enriched by reading the interviews.

To Your Victory and Success

Bro. Bedford

Foreword by

Robert L. Johnson, Founder of BET
Founder & Chairman, The RLJ Companies

I have been asked on more than one occasion over the life of my career, "How do I become a successful entrepreneur and are there any books I would recommend to achieve entrepreneurial success?"

I have repeatedly stressed how you can generate value by creating a brand identity that helps you generate deal opportunities. You should look for sectors that are growing and identify strategic partners who can bring something to the deal that you don't such as capital, talent, and infrastructure.

The answer to the second half of that question is there isn't any one book that can give you everything you need to know about being a successful entrepreneur.

However, I will say that the best way to get you started on your journey of entrepreneurship is to learn from those who have already gone down the road before you. Learn from those who have left footprints.

In Conversations with Black Millionaire Entrepreneurs you'll get real life changing information from some of the most successful black entrepreneurs in America today. All in one source, all at the same time.

Although I didn't have a book like this when I started, I believe it is a valuable resource for those who are striving to become successful entrepreneurs.

Bro. Bedford has provided a tremendous service to the African-American community with these interviews.

'Entrepreneurship: My Conversations with Black Millionaire Entrepreneurs' is not just a book, but also a valuable guide and resource for those looking to achieve wealth and success.

Conversation with Les Brown

Bro. Bedford (BB): This is Bro. Bedford from The Association of Black Entrepreneurs and I am just overjoyed with who is joining me in conversation today. This gentleman has risen into international prominence by delivering a high-energy message that tells people, how to shake off **mediocrity** and live up to their greatness. His message is not one of theory; here is a man that actually practices what he preaches. He is an internationally recognized speaker.

He is also the author of the highly acclaimed and successful books, *Live Your Dreams* and the recently released; *It's Not Over Until You Win*. He hosted a national syndicated talk show, which focused on solutions rather than problems. He's one of the world's leading authorities in understanding and stimulating human potential.

I can go on and on about business accolades and awards this gentleman has received throughout the years. He's the one and only, world-renowned speaker, successful entrepreneur, best-selling author, radio and television celebrity, Mr. Les Brown.

Thank you for joining us today.

Les Brown: Well thank you so much and you proved that $5 can go a long way. I'm going to give you $6 next time for that build up all right.

Bro Bedford: (Laughter). I am truly honored. You are truly one of my heroes as it relates to successful black entrepreneurs. As I started compiling these interviews, I knew that this series would not be complete without your voice being added to this series. So I thank you once again. I am truly honored.

Les Brown: Well thank you so much for having me, sir.

Bro. Bedford: Yes sir. Well let's get started because I do know you're a very busy man. How did you get your start as an entrepreneur?

Les Brown: Well we all know that it all starts with a decision that we want to be our own boss and it's something what want to do, we want to do it our way and go into the market place and test ourselves with our products, our services or our information.

I decided that speaking was an arena that I love the business of it, I love changing people's lives and I wanted to take on the challenge of going into this industry where I had no experience and no prior knowledge of what it would take to do it, something that was very challenging and establish myself as the intellectual resource for corporate America.

This was twenty (20) years ago. There was no such thing as an African American motivational speaker, Black motivational speaker. So at that time to want to get a $1K per hour to train white corporate America, how to achieve their corporate goals was just not done. It was not something that most people had envisioned and that's what I set out to do.

In our community, if you have a desire to help people, because of our conditioning and because of past experiences in our history, we chose to become ministers. I think that's why we have more churches and ministers than we have businesses because that was the first avenue of expression.

But this was some area that had never been carved out. A brother motivating corporate America, so I like that kind of stuff. (Laughter) I was gonna motivate the man.

Bro Bedford: (laughter)

Les Brown: (Laughter); so it was fun and it has been fun. It's been a great ride for twenty years and I've earned just over $52 million dollars and it's been a fascinating, enlightening and empowering experience.

Bro Bedford: Yes sir. I'm sure just as you mentioned going into to white corporate America and motivating them, I'm sure that was a serious challenge. But I want to ask you what where some of the major challenges that you faced or that you had to overcome in your beginning stages as an entrepreneur?

Les Brown: Well one of the first things I had to do was I had to sale myself on that. One of the things that I would suggest is, are you open to some coaching?

Bro Bedford: Yes. Absolutely.

4

Les Brown: One of the things I suggest that you do is drop the title "Black Entrepreneur".

Bro Bedford: Uh hum!

Les Brown: I had to begin to face something that my mentor said to me. He said, "Les, you're more than you're paint job and if you see yourself as a black entrepreneur, then they will see you how you see yourself and how you see yourself connects with the history they have about black entrepreneurs.

You have got to position yourselves as you are the one and your message is for the planet and knowledge and your expertise and your level competence and your confidence as you bring it forth, that they'll forgot about your paint job based upon your content and your character and deal with you because you can impact their bottom line.

You've got to out work them and out think them but there cannot be in your thinking "I would like for you to do business with me because I'm a black entrepreneur and so on". Because that doesn't work at the level you want to go to.

I don't speak at black history time and Dr. Martin Luther King's birthday, I speak all year long. And so, I get $25K an hour speaking domestically to corporations and $55K internationally.

And so at that level, doing that three to four times per week and having the reputation for specializing and custom designing a presentation to meet the needs of corporations. Going up against major firms not having their PowerPoint presentations, not having the MBA's and PhD's and competing against them on a yearly basis.

Usually, if they see my name on a roster for a contract they usually come and talk to me about sub-contracting with them because they know I most certainly will get it.

And so, it's about …

1) How you vision yourself, having a larger vision of yourself beyond your paint job and seeing yourself as a force to be reckoned with on the planet, that's number one. And…

2) Holding yourself to a higher standard that they don't because in order for us to be considered average we have to be extraordinary. We have to be at least five to ten times better we can't just be as good as; we have to be better than.

And so, the whole regiment that I went through to train myself so that

1) The fact that I happen to be black,

2) The fact that I never worked for a major corporation,

3) That fact that I don't have any major college education,

4) That I had no track record of achievement in this area,

5) I had no recommendations and had no colleague or anyone to point me out and say, he can do this and was asking for a $1K an hour to motivate corporations to do something I had never done and ask them to fill out an evaluation form to tell me what they want me to tell them.

Now to me when I call the psychic hotline and they ask me what's my name? I say well you tell me. (Laughter) so to me when I look back, I said Aretha Franklin used to have a song called "How I Got Over" and sometimes I look back and I wonder, how I got over? (Laughter) I can sing that song! Yes!

And let me share something with you.

Bro. Bedford: Sure.

Les Brown: As entrepreneurs, there are five things that are indispensable for making it in the global economy:

1. **Is your mindset.**

I cannot tell you how important that is that you work on that on a regular basis. Your mindset is crucial when you are in business. And just to deal with the <u>emotional</u>, <u>stressful</u>, <u>unpredictable</u>, <u>volatile</u> environment that you just don't know what's going to happen from one minute to the next.

Bro. Bedford: Uh hum!

Les Brown: There are many people between you and the money and people you have to depend upon. I used to be insulted, when I would hear years ago, white people, when they were asked about why don't you have blacks working and they would say well send me some that are qualified and want to work.

I used to be insulted by that, now, you ask me (laughter) aren't you going to hire some brothers and sisters, send me some who are qualified and who want to work. I'm here to tell you, it's amazing how people just want a paycheck. They don't want to work.

In the twenty years I've been doing this, I've earned just over $52 million dollars. That's crumbs! Had I not been narrow in my thinking; I should have selected people, not based upon their paint job to formulate my team. I should have selected them based upon their competence and their being in the business…

Bro. Bedford: Uh hum!

Les Brown…and partnering with me and growing with me because I out grew the team I had for a long time. And now at this stage in my life, I'm an old man now, I'm sixty-three. The fact that I can do a 140 push-ups non-stop does not erase the fact that I'm old now. I forget that because of my energy and because of what I'm doing now. I'm still excited about what I'm doing because this is not work. The only part that's work is getting ready to go to the airport.

That's what I charge them for. The speech is free, I charge them $25K to go through the airport and get another prostate examination. That's what I charge them for. (Laughter).

Bro. Bedford: Right!.

Les Brown: But as I'm looking at my life, I'll give you case-in-point; usually in the month of December, the speaking business and training business usually is very slow. It's around Christmas time and so you might do $30-40K dollars max that month and that's a good month.

Bro. Bedford: Uh hum!

Les Brown: In an hour and a half because of the strategic relationship and as a result of the strategic relationship, it gave me access to a market that I did not have access to. I learned the process of how to deliver a sales presentation that I did not know before then. In an hour and a half, I earned $410K dollars

Bro. Bedford: Uh hum.

Les Brown: Okay. What was changed? Same person, twenty years in the industry a different relationship, a different team that the difference of being in the business and the business being in you that introduced me to strategies and a process that I was not aware of because I got on this track twenty years ago and one of the things that's very important is:

1) Working on your mindset

2) Making sure you stay ahead of the game in terms of your learning and being a master in this arena

3) Surrounding yourself with people who are continuously in-volved with

      a. growing and staying ahead of you.

That's the mistake that I made. I didn't do that. Now I understand that when I was on a board with T.D. Jakes. He came into the room and he said, good evening it's so great to see all of you hear. Let me put this out here, as soon as I know as much as the rest of you around this table, you're fired and I'll get another group.

That was a strong statement. People laughed nervously, but now I understand that you have to have people around you that know more than you.

Bro Bedford: Uh hum.

Les Brown: And as soon as you know as much as they know, you no longer need them. I had people around me where I knew more than them. It was Dennis Kimbro, who wrote *"Think And Grow Rich, a Black Choice"*, he said if you're the smartest one in your group you need to get a new group.

Bro. Bedford: Uh hum.

Les Brown: So I was the smartest one in my group and I did not know what a liability that was to me business wise. You have to have people who know more than you and who are continuously growing, staying ahead of the game and bringing you stuff as opposed to you bringing them stuff.

The other thing that's very, very important as an entrepreneur that most people and particularly African Americans, don't invest in…I'm about to get off this call and I've been on a call with this company called American Home Mortgage and they have a national corporation.

That has been an advantage for me in dealing in the market that I deal in because 99% of my customers are white; and that is mindset, working on yourself on a regular basis, listening to motivation messages, reading positive material to reprogram your mind to overcome the subtle, unconscious mental conditioning that keeps us from playing on a high level and it just creeps back in. And I'll give you some examples if we have the time.

But the other thing that's very important is investing in your communication skills. Put your money where your mouth is. It gives you your ability to communicate because I did that and I still do that.

I trained last year just over five thousand doctors. I taught them how to communicate with their patients and to increase their patients' compliance in taking their hypertension medication. That was 30 minutes a day, Monday thru Thursday, a $640K dollar contract.

Bro Bedford: Uh hum.

Les Brown: Thirty minutes a day, 12 (noon) until 12:30 p.m.; four days a week. (Laughter). I've never been a doctor and I never had a patient.

How did I beat out all of these other white firms?

Not only was I able to express and connect with the pharmaceutical company that was going to release the contract, but I conducted **communications intelligence.** Unlike my white competitors who came there with an idea of what it took to teach these doctors how to communicate with their patients.

I spent a lot of time finding patients who were taking their medications and asked what role their doctors played in doing that. I talked to patients who were doing it, to find out or to give me a portrait of the personality and the style of the doctor, his staff and his practice and what role that played in them being cooperative in the process.

Bro. Bedford: Uh hum.

Les Brown: As well as talked to doctors who felt that they were successful in getting their patients to take their medications. That was the heart and soul of my presentation. The insights that I brought, made them know, even though I didn't have an MBA, even though I have no health care training whatsoever in my background that this man knows what he's talking about. And I got the contract.

Bro Bedford: Question, excuse me. I heard you a couple of years ago and I heard you say that you had succeeded as a speaker, but you had failed at the speaking business. Is that when you made that transformation?

Les Brown: Absolutely! I've made over $52 million dollars not knowing what the hell I was doing.

Bro Bedford: Laughter

Les Brown: Yeah, yeah and the reason is because right now as late as Saturday, Saturday. I was in Summerset, New Jersey training a guy named T. Harv Eker's speakers and trainers on how to tell stories and position your story so it has value for an audience and to move them, to motivate them, to persuade them to get them to make the choices that you want them to make.

I got up early that morning to go down and see what was going on before me. They were doing a training called, *How to Present the Irresistible Sale*.

Bro. Bedford: Uh hum.

Les Brown: They gave the top ten secrets of guys that I work with that because I've known them for years and we speak in different places and very seldom we are in the same place unless we're on stage then we speak and we run and we're gone. So I got a chance to see all of these various presentations and some I had seen before, but now looking at them from the inside out finding out why the work.

I had eighty people to speak to. I was there going through the training with them. I came up on the stage, I stayed in the room, did not leave, came up on the stage to do my presentation and then paused in my presentation because I had an hour and a half to do but I had to catch a plane and planes had been cancelled coming into Chicago, so I had to cut it to forty-five minutes. So I said, well let's see how well I learned the irresistible sale and people began to laugh in the audience.

Now mind you, for twenty years, I prided myself on two things: 1) Being the highest paid speaker at $25K per hour. The only people that earn more than I do are guys like Gullianni out of New York; former President Clinton; Zig Ziggler earns like around $11K; Jack Canfield, $20K; Mark Victor Hansen, who co-wrote Chicken Soup For the Soul, those guys get around $10K. But most of the celebrity speakers taper off around $10K-$15K highest. I get $25K for thirty minutes and sometimes I've spoken for less as five minutes, flew to Hawaii and spoke for five minute, four minutes and they paid me $25K dollars and I left. (Laughter) four minutes...

Bro. Bedford: Laughter,

Les Brown: Because the people ahead of me went over. But internationally, I charge $55K, plus they usually have me with seven interpreters. Next week, I'm going to Ottawa, Canada, Calgary and speaking to over six thousand entrepreneurs there.

But what happened was, here I am priding myself as being one of the highest paid speakers on the planet and T. Harv trains his people, not to get a fee. Wow! I'm saying whoa, what does he mean by that? And then here I pride myself as getting more standing ovations than anybody in the industry and here he is training his people not to get a standing ovation. He trains his people to get a running ovation to the back of the room to buy products. I said whoa!

That presentation because I changed and used the running ovation strategy and they knew I was going to do it. I talked about it at each step, now I'm going to do this, he told us to do this. They knew the steps, the elements to drive them to the back of the room and they still got up and went back there and bought over a $130K dollars' worth of products.

Blew me away! Eighty people! Eighty people! So the lesson in that is Dwight Pledge, one of the speakers I'm training now is… doing it is not, I love the excitement of going to Ottawa, Canada or speaking to American Home this morning and blowing their minds. I like that. I like it when I come in the room and they look and they know he doesn't play football, he's not a basketball player, he doesn't sing, he doesn't dance, but he's about to make our nose bleed. Okay. (Laughter)

Bro. Bedford: Laughter.

Les Brown: I like the voice in my head. This priest, this Catholic Priest was at an event where I spoke and he said, what a paradox, God has raised from among his oppressed a motivator to motivate his oppressor. (Laughter).

Bro. Bedford: Laughter.

Les Brown: I like it when they give me that check and I run to the bank speaking in unknown tongues (laugher)

Bro Bedford: (laughter)

Les Brown: It's so much fun because the looks on some people's faces are like what are you going to do? Who are you? And just to break them down, I like that. I like it, write this down. I like that.

Bro. Bedford: Right, right.

Les Brown: My challenge is now, what turns me on now, that's okay, but what turns me on now is training others to do it and I've got some speakers now that's giving the old man a run for his money.

And I like teaching and training people how to negotiate how to develop their leadership potential, how to impact the sales process, build relationships and quadruple your income in any industry, how to establish a brand, a reputation and dominate your niche. That's what my goal was when I came into this industry. To dominate it and that's what I do.

Now I'm learning the business. I dominate the speaking aspect of it. That's a different mindset. I'm learning the business; I'm now working with a person like T. Harv Eker, who's earned over 200 million dollars in a year.

Bro Bedford: Uh hum

Les Brown: Well I hear people say; well he's white, no that's not the biggie, so what. This is an area where we have an advantage. He has a process and he has a team of people that know some stuff that I don't know. And now I probably will have about 1/3 of his team who volunteered to come work with me. Many of them are going to put in there resignation to come and work with me because they like the way I do business and how I operate.

That's going to take my stuff. I will probably do what took me twenty years to do, with this new team that I've assembled and they've got a brother up in there too and a sister. I saw them, they're coming. It will probably take me less than 15 months with the knowledge that they're bringing.

Bro. Bedford: That took you twenty years.

Les Brown: took me twenty years, yes. Twenty years. But I don't care. 52 million dollars, a good God and a healthy heart and you can make it through the winter in Miami, FL. (laughter)

Bro. Bedford: That's right, that's right

Les Brown: I'm telling you, my brother.

Bro. Bedford: I know you have to go. Can I ask one more Question?

Les Brown: Go ahead, I can talk to you, go ahead.

Bro. Bedford: Okay, You spoke about the importance of speaking and communication as an entrepreneur and I think you touched on that beautifully. In connection with that what is the most important trait or characteristic that a young brother or sister must have if they're on the track of entrepreneurship?

Les Brown: And that is a belief in themselves, see communication skills are important, but who you are behind the words that's far more important than the words themselves. Because under every deal, underneath every conversation, underneath every presentation, there's the energy, there's your conviction, there's your character, there's your spirit.

And for you to convince someone to hire you, to consult with you, to accept you as the vendor that they're going to do business with, that connection, that decision cannot just be cerebral it just can't be based upon the numbers.

I deliberately charge more money than everyone else. And so, I'm making a statement about my stuff. Oh you want something cheaper, fantastic. I can get you a $10K speaker. I just happen not to be the one. I train them and I know a lot of them and let me give you their numbers.

Bro Bedford: Uh hum.

Les Brown: Gladly, because I have over 3K request a month, I mean a year and so I'm not out looking for business, I don't generate business, business comes to me.

You do that through holding yourself to a higher standard operating out of the thinking of Henry David Thoreau, who said "*do not go where the path may lead, but go where there's no path and leave a trail*".

The regiment in which I train myself and in which I'm now training and putting together a structure to train my speakers on, a regiment that my competition cannot even respond to because they didn't train themselves like I train myself.

They didn't have to they had privilege. 87% of what they want is available to them because they have the complexion of connection. I didn't have that. So I had to train myself in a different kind of regiment.

They can go up give the same speech for 30 years and regurgitate that "*one speech fits all situations*". I didn't have that option being black. So I had to train myself in a different kind of way. They operate out of the thinking of the Dale Carnegie course, which is a great course, tell them what you're going to tell them, tell them, and then tell them what you've told them.

I couldn't do that. I have to go from a different place. I train my speakers to conduct communication intelligence. My favorite book says, "In all thy getting, get understanding". Find out who they are.

Bro. Bedford: Uh hum

Les Brown: Once you find out who they are, craft a message in a language in which they can relate to. Don't let what you want to say get in the way of what they need to hear so that you can make impact, because **impact drives income**.

And because of that standard that I train myself on, they can't do that. They just can't go up on a stage and start speaking on any subject matter in any industry and command the kind of money that I get.

I'm training my speakers to be flexible and versatile to do that on any industry, period. Five minutes prep, and they'll think you're the expert for the hour that you talk. So we always have to hold ourselves to a higher standard, when it comes to the knowledge because **knowledge is the new currency** and coming to express it, to communicate it, to relate to different people on different levels.

Once you open your mouth, that person is making an assessing of you.

Bro. Bedford: Uh hum

Les Brown: So this voice that you here was not always here. By being trained by Mike Williams, who's been my mentor for the past 37 years, out of Columbus, OH, who was born in Coshocton, OH. This brother, who dropped out of Ohio State University, trained and mentored me over the years.

He was my newsman and was a community activist during the sixties and I admired him. He was a speaker then and I was one of his groupies and went around watching him and studying his style. I was fascinated with it. He had a big Afro and we called him treetop. Big huge Afro.

Both: Laughter

Les Brown: Like Angela Davis type. Then he came to the station working as a newsman and between the records, convinced me that I can be more than a disc jockey, more than the man about town, Les

Brown, more than LB, triple p, Les Brown, your planet plan popper, that I can communicate to the planet. He went about the business of teaching me and here we are the rest is history.

Bro. Bedford: That's a wonderful history. I'm sure that many of our subscribers and hopefully those who will begin to subscribe will really appreciate your message. Can you tell the subscribers and the listeners, how they can get in contact with you and get a hold of this wonderful training that you have?

Les Brown: Mike Williams and I, we do the training ourselves. In fact, next year because of T. Harv Eker, I said oh my God He said Les, did you notice that out of eighty people, sixty three (63) signed up for your speaker training? I said yes. He said, "it's four days". I said, yes. He said, Les you charged $2500 dollars. He said, that's too cheap, that's too cheap. He said, we give four day training and they give $20K a head, it's too cheap. So, people who are coming, they better hurry up.

Both: Laughter

Les Brown: Laughter: because it's going up my goodness gracious. I said, Oh No! They have sold out. I probably have, if I'm lucky. They're trying to get another room. We probably have about five seats available because they bought them out.

They want to know how could he do this, not knowing the business. They know I don't know. They know I'm not joking because they ask me questions and they can't believe that they don't know this. (Laughter) How did you get here? I said, I don't know.

But there are some things that I do know that I focus on. 1). What was my strength? What were their weaknesses? And how can I exploit that and make that my strength? I was thinking in terms of dominating the market.

When Toastmasters International did a poll of 51,000 members worldwide to select the five top speakers in the world, they selected General Norman Swartzkoff, Barbara Walters, Robert Schuler, Paul Harvey and myself. I got more votes than all of them combined, which was a great honor. And was selected by the National Speakers Association for the Speaker's Hall of Fame, it's called a CPAE Award, where you're selected by your peers.

To me my goal was/is to create a path for other African-Americans to come down and once getting here to train them because now you learn, you earn and you pass it on. Now that I'm in my Colonel Sanders years, it's time to pass it on to others and that's what we're doing in my training summits.

Success is not convenient. Seize the moment.

Bro. Bedford: They can go to www.lesbrown.com?

Les Brown: If they want to sign up, what I'll do for a special for you as entrepreneurs, it's $2500. If they call you, you call me and give me their information, well give them a $500 discount.

Bro. Bedford: Yes, sir! You also have a cruise coming up as well.

Les Brown: I have a cruise once a year comes up, *Cruise Your Way to Greatness*. On this cruise, we'll share with people, the many strategies to creating multiple streams of income and how to...we're doing a piece called Put Your Money Where Your Mouth Is. Another one is *How to Leverage and Build Relationships Beyond Our Community*.

The other one that is very important is Balance. How do you make it in a world where in many cases there are some people taking care of their parents while their taking care of their kids and run a business. And you have a kid that decides to go crazy, you know. How do you maintain sanity in insane situations? And there are some strategies.

It's some of the things that I've learned that I think will be helpful to them. How do you handle it when you're an entrepreneur and someone in your family has been diagnosed with an illness?

Or you've been told you have cancer, like I was ten years ago and so you got two or three years. I beat those odds and saw it as a project as opposed to a death sentence. So those are some of the things we're going to deal with. They can go to our website and register for that as well.

Bro. Bedford: Okay and get all of your books and audios at the website?

Les Brown: Yes, tell them that if they're serious. This is just for people that are serious. There's a set of CD's called *Choosing Your Future*. It's the best work I've done and I like them and I don't like them because I don't think I've done anything that's superior to those yet. It's a six-week series that was going to be the last tapes that I was going to do before venturing into television. But the venture into television didn't last as long as I thought it was going to. We're doing something now. But *Choosing Your Future*, you can get that one online.

The other one is called, *Presentation Power, Part I & II*. That's a must for everybody's library that's an entrepreneur because it teaches how to communicate on the phone, small settings one-on-one and larger groups.

I've spoken to over 80,000 in the Georgia Dome. So I teach you things that I've learned not from the books but from university of hard knocks, but that's what I teach.

This takes you up and beyond "The Secret". Everybody is talking about "The Secret". *The Secret* works very well for white folks.

Bro. Bedford: Laughter

Les Brown: But the stuff that we need, it's above and beyond. In fact, I'm going to do a book called Above And Beyond, The Secret. You know because when we come in there is no secret. (Laughter)

Bro. Bedford: Right.

Les Brown: Yeah, we aren't going to get the business, okay. Let me give you an example. Here in Chicago, just imagine talking about mental conditioning, Chicago, once was considered a very progressive city. Right now it's a mayor's election. Where do you live?

Bro. Bedford: I'm in Detroit.

Les Brown: Okay. Chicago has 52% of Black registered voters. Fifty-two percent of the voters are Black and they voted a higher percentage than whites. White people in Chicago represent 30% of the vote. Now twenty years ago, when Mayor Harold Washington was in office, black people got 44% of the contracts of a 2 Billion dollar budget. Twenty years later Mayor Daley elected with 80% of the black vote with two black people running against him. Not one black leader endorsed these two black people. One person, Dorothy Brown, is a clerk of court, she's an attorney, she's an MBA and she is a Certified Public Accountant. He (Mayor Daley) was elected with over 80% of the black vote.

Now let's look at the contracts, twenty years later what percentage of the contracts do you think that black people get? Now they got 44% twenty years ago under Harold Washington who was elected with the black vote. What percentage do you think they get now with over 80% of the black vote for Mayor Richard Daley?

Bro. Bedford: I'm going to jump out there and say probably less than 25%.

Les Brown: Black people get 6% of the contracts. White contractors get 92%, Latino's get 2% and Black contractors get 6%.

Bro Bedford: That is a drastic, 6% that is a drastic drop.

Les Brown: Yes indeed.

Bro Bedford: Drastic.

Les Brown: Yes indeed

Bro. Bedford: Paradigm shift right, is that a paradigm shift?

Les Brown: That's not a paradigm shift, that's mental conditioning. You have to get underneath that. The level of self-loathing and self-hatred, that has to be interrupted. What people do, what they produce is the result of the conversation they believe about themselves.

And so, getting underneath that stuff and giving them a larger vision of themselves and empowering them to break through the good ole boys network Mindset of we're going to take care of a few, and you few, you control the masses.

Bro Bedford: Uh hum

Les Brown: Yeah, it's quite an interesting thing. Quite interesting indeed. Fascinating to watch this stuff.

Bro. Bedford: Sounds like we have a challenge ahead of us.

Les Brown: Oh without question. I think it's very exciting and I'd like the opportunity to deal with it and I probably, but I got to first go and get this money. Laughter

Bro. Bedford: Laughter

Les Brown: I got to get this money right now. I got another goal over here that's got me real excited where I can make more money at home than on the road. I like that one.

Bro. Bedford: Yes, yes. We probably are going to have to bring you back on to talk about that sometime soon.

Les Brown: Oh man, there's so much money. This is a 58 Billion dollar industry. This is an industry, just think about this. We're the only people that have more churches than we have businesses.

Bro. Bedford: umm

Les Brown: More ministers than we have entrepreneurs. We have the highest poverty rate, the highest incarceration rate, and highest crime rate. For every African-American Male that goes to college, one hundred go to jail

Bro. Bedford: umm

Les Brown: Okay. So as we look at ourselves looking into the future, we have to incorporate spirituality with practicality.

Bro. Bedford: Uh hum.

Les Brown: Bill Gates says the retraining of Americans will be the biggest budget in this century. We're going through something that the media doesn't talk about. It's called the three (3) P's: Purchase, Power, and Parity.

The belief is that over the next 10 to 15 to 20 years as we now are moving forward into the global economy, *American workers will have to do more, do it faster, do it better with less resources and permanent part-time employees with no health benefits*.

Eventually they hope to achieve in 15 to 20 years, a level economic

20

playing field because the only countries that we are in war with are poor countries. We're not in war with any wealthy countries. Poor countries are what we're in war with.

So when they say we are twenty-five thousand people working for a corporation and they layoff ten thousand people. Those ten thousand jobs don't go away they spread those ten thousand jobs among the fifteen thousand that's still there.

Bro. Bedford: Uh hum

Les Brown: Now that introduces a speaker. Now comes on the stage a trainer because now they need to be trained on how to _do more_, _do it faster_.

They need to be trained on how to develop their leadership potential, that fifteen thousand that's still there. They need to be trained how to accommodate those new ten thousand jobs. They need to be trained how to raise the level of morale and give people a sense of certainty in an uncertain situation where there's no such thing as job security.

They need to be trained how to optimize the efficiency of the operation and how to create a shift in the mindset of people so they don't think in terms of sabotaging the company and come back and shooting people and going postal.

They need to be trained on how to accommodate this level of transformation that's taking place, this level of work and feel good about it.

Bro. Bedford: Uh hum

Les Brown: That's where we get paid $25K an hour to do.

Bro. Bedford: Training.

Les Brown : Yes, sir.

BB: Yes, sir.

LB: Let the record show. As I'm telling you it's a serious business up in here and one of the few areas that I know that being an African-American, being a black man is an advantage.

Because when Tony Robbins, or Zig Ziggler or Jack Canfield or *Chicken Soup for the Soul* goes on stage and says you have the power to live your dreams, they look at him and they look at themselves and say, if he can do it, I can do it. But when you and I go on stage and say, you have the power to live your dream, they look at you and think about our history and look at themselves and say, if he can do it, I know damn well I can do it. Let me get the hell out of here now **(laughter to loud-Smile)**

BB: Laughter

LB: As they leave there running.

Both laugh

LB: It's fun man I tell you.

Bro. Bedford: I can hear that you are having just a ball doing what you do and that's one of the most powerful characteristic that I like, I love about you. The energy and the excitement that you bring to what you do.

Les Brown: You know what's exciting to me now? Training somebody, giving them everything I know to beat me. That's the most fascinating thing. When I'm on the road, I had one of the most powerful moments in my life as a speaker, when two weeks ago, one of my speakers spoke after I spoke, Ed Blunt out of New York.

He's been in training for two years. A lady came up to me and said, "I hope I don't hurt your feeling by what I'm going to say". I said, not all. She said, we don't need you anymore, we've got Ed.

I said, well thank you very much. (Laughter)

BB: Laughter

Les Brown: That was the greatest compliment I have ever gotten as a coach. People say that after my daughter speaks or Ed Blunt, Kevin Bracey, Johnny Wimbrey, Erika McKay or any of the other speakers. They always say that. I mean my top sixteen, and that to me is (pause while a conversation is going on with people in Les' office) a great compliment.

LB: Yeah

22

BB: I'm sure you have to go, correct?

LB: Yeah, but go ahead, you want to ask me another question?

BB: I just want to thank you. I mean you've given such a wealth of knowledge and again I will do some…

LB: You're a goldmine. Listening to you, what a great voice. You're a goldmine, man

BB: Well I'm coming to you.

LB: You aught to come down there man in Orlando, FL.

BB: I will be there. I will be there. The other thing that I'm doing, I've interviewed Dennis Kimbro,

LB: Yeah,

BB: I'm glad you mentioned him

LB: He is so talented.

BB: George Fraser,

LB: Oh yeah, George Fraser, yes.

BB: Cathy Hughes, the great Cathy Hughes

LB: Uh hum.

BB: And of course in doing what I'm doing, my whole ambition is to lead people to you all. You all are like the hidden treasures. Every time I'm doing presentations, I always ask, do you have *Think And Grow Rich*, in your library, and to my surprise, no*! Do you have Success Runs in Our Race?* No!

Les Brown: Uh hum.

Bro. Bedford: Have you had any CD or motivational tape by Les Brown, and no!

Les Brown: Umm

Bro. Bedford: So that's really my mission I believe is to make sure that we amplify those who have already been there and done that.

Les Brown: Yes Absolutely.

Bro. Bedford: I really want to lead people to you.

Les Brown: And that's how we grow.

Bro. Bedford: Um hum.

Les Brown: Well I appreciate it. Thank you. I look forward to working with you.

Bro. Brown: I look forward to working with you too.

Les Brown: Thank you and God bless you.

Bro. Bedford: Thank you, sir and God bless you.

Conversation with Cathy Hughes

Bro. Bedford: This is Bro. Bedford, from the Association Of Black Entrepreneurs and I am extremely excited at about who is joining me today in conversation. Joining me today is the **Founder and Chairperson of Radio One, Inc.**, **the largest African-American Broadcast Company in the nation.**

Radio One is the first African-American company in radio history to dominate several major markets simultaneously and possesses the first woman owned radio station to rank number one in any major market.

In 1995, Radio One purchased WKYS in Washington, D.C for $40 million dollars, the largest transaction between two black companies in broadcasting history. In 1999, when Radio One went public, Ms. Hughes made history again by becoming the **first African-American woman with a company on the stock exchange.**

Radio One's value is currently in excess of $2 billion dollars. Black Enterprise named Radio One the company of the year. Fortune rated it one of the 100 best companies to work for and Radio One was inducted into the Maryland Business Hall of Fame.

Recently, Radio One entered into another venture starting TV One. According to Black Enterprise, TV One in 2006 was the fastest growing network. Her pioneering work has lead Essence to name her one of the hundred who have changed the world and one of the most powerful and influential persons.

Radio Inc. continues to list her as one of the twenty most influential women in radio. Ebony sites her as one of the ten most powerful women in Black America. I can go on, and on and on with all of the business accolades and awards that she has received but we wouldn't have time for this interview.

So without further delay, I would like to thank you, the incomparable and the matchless, Ms. Cathy Hughes. Thank you for joining us.

Cathy Hughes: Thank you Bro. Bedford, the reason that the introduction is so long isn't because of my accomplishments it's because of my age. After you live so long it just gets longer and longer. I've been blessed by God to serve my people and I thank you for this opportunity to share my story with your readers.

Bro Bedford: Oh, thank you very much and I know you don't have a lot of time so we'll get right to the questions. How did you get your start as an entrepreneur?

Cathy Hughes: Well number one; I'm a third generation entrepreneur. It's kind of in my blood. My family has always worked for themselves. My grandfather, well I'm actually a fourth generation now that I think about it because my grandfather's family were also entrepreneurs.

When it's in your DNA, it's just a matter of time before you have to do it. For one thing your family is kind of judgmental about you working for other people. Most of them have needs in their businesses so if you're not going to work for yourself, then you need to come and help them out.

I always knew that ultimately I would work for myself. The way it actually occurred was I had created a program called *"The Quiet Storm"* which went on to become the number one format in the history of urban radio.

I was stolen away from Howard University, where I created this format by a group of thirty-six stock holders in a company that was fifteen years old and had been trying unsuccessfully the entire time of its existence and had gone through millions of dollars, to get a dark signal back on the air in broadcasting.

Well I was successful in doing that for them. I got them on the air. I completely staffed the facility. I named it and I picked the format. I did everything from soup to nuts, A to Z and then they ran out of money. Well I have never had, thank God, thank God, had a paycheck to bounce. I believe that if a person works for you, if somebody is not going to be paid, it should be you, not them. I had literally started to use my retirement money to pay my staff because the company had run out of money.

I went to them and said, "*You all need an infusion of capital*". They said, "*We want you to put together a proposal and go and shop for a loan for us*". I said, "*excuse me, I'm a General Manager, I'm not an owner of this company and if I go out and secure a loan for you* which is outside my area of responsibility, I think that I should be entitled to an equity stake in your company."

Well they laughed at me. The youngest person on this board was seventy years old at this time and I was probably thirty-eight or thirty-nine. So to them I was a young arrogant whippersnapper, with a lot of mouth. They said, "*No we're not sharing. We've been together for fifteen years; you don't know the sacrifices we've been through.*"

So I'm like yeah, but it wasn't productive. I'm the one who got you on the air. One word led to another and they said, "*Well if you think you know so much, you need to go and buy your own radio station*". **Well boom, it was like a light bulb went off in my head.**

It dawned upon me, how stupid was I being. This group of distinguished individuals, thirty-six of them thought that I had the ability to get them a loan. So if they had that level of confidence in me securing a loan, I should be able to do that for myself.

I need to have more confidence in Cathy Hughes and I thanked them. I started putting my things in my briefcase and they said, "*What are you doing*?" **Resigning!** They said, "*Why are you resigning*?" I said, "*Because you told me; I need to go and get myself a loan because I need to buy a radio station*". And that's how I became an entrepreneur.

I say to young entrepreneurs and young people all the time; sometimes what you think is your darkest hour, is in fact the blessing that God had intended for you to receive. But we don't see it because we want something else and we're so hell bent on doing it our way and getting what we want, but we don't see what God has in store for us.

On that day I'm telling you it was as if the heavens had opened up and I saw it crystal clear.

Bro Bedford: That is such a wonderful story and as you were telling it, I of course read your history and I noted that there were some challenges when you went out to acquire your station. What were some of the major challenges that you faced in your beginning?

Cathy Hughes: I was black. I was female and I was considered young.

Bro. Bedford: All of which you could not change.

Cathy Hughes: Yes all of which I could not change and I was in the child bearing age. I can't tell you how many bankers said to me, "*you might get pregnant*". Yeah, well what does that have to do with you loaning me a million dollars. I had more male bankers spend more time questioning me about my personal life than I did talking to me about my business **acumen**

At that time I didn't realize and again I say this to entrepreneurs, this is so critical. **You have to have a productive working relationship with a bank.** When you don't have and most African American do not have a close relationship with a bank.

Black preachers are the worst. On Monday morning they put hundreds of millions of dollars collectively into these banks around the country. And then when they want to build anything new, they have to go and beg for a loan.

They don't have relationships with a bank where they can say all right not only am I going to take my money out of here but I'm going to get ten other preachers in this city to take their money out of here too.

Black people don't realize the importance and I didn't at that time. *I had no idea that more often than not in securing financing, it's based on a relationship*. **It's not based on a business plan**. **It's not based on the dream or the vision you have and it's not based on your credentials**. In so many of these situations, *it's based on a relationship that somebody already has with a lending institution.*

Bro. Bedford: I get that question a lot. Just this morning, I received a couple of emails from individuals and that was their main question. How do I go about acquiring financing to get started or to do this or to do that?

Cathy Hughes: Absolutely.

Bro. Bedford: Yes so a relationship has to be built.

Cathy Hughes: A quick story, I had been in business for about eight or nine months, it was my first year. Within ninety days of me going into business the prime went into the mid-twenties and my senior loan with Chemical Bank of New York was 2.5 points over prime. For one of those quarters my interest rate was at 28.25%, can you imagine?

Anyway, a long story, short. I'm concerned about payroll because I'm trying to keep up my loan payments and my revenue or my cash flow hasn't started to really be adequate to cover my expenses. I go to my bank where I had already deposited about 7 or 8 hundred thousand dollars over that time period and told them that I needed a $10K loan.

I had a 10k short fall on payroll that I was concerned about and I needed a temporary $10K loan. I showed them a contract from an advertiser. I had $32K coming from an advertiser at that time, it was just not going to hit my account in a timely fashion to make sure that my payroll checks were secure and they told me no.

They would not loan me $10K. I could not tell you, how again the heavens parted and light bulbs went off in my head. I realized that if had been standing in front of that loan officer asking for $30-40 thousand dollars to buy a Mercedes Benz, they wouldn't have blinked, okay.

I could buy any car I wanted for any amount of money I wanted, but they would not give me, a black businessperson $10,000 to make certain that my payroll was secured and covered, when I had a contract that showed them that I had $32K coming in within the next 30 days. **Again, I realized relationship.**

Once I got the relationship, I love to tell this story. My lease was up on a building and I needed to move. A banker whom I did not know, a woman named Karen Calious, who was one of my listeners to my morning show.

At that time, I was doing everything, hosting the morning show and running the company. She realized that I was very close to losing a location for my facility because the District of Columbia, where I was located was supposed to be making one of these small business loans available to me and they didn't.

I had gone to closing on the building I needed to move into twice and both times they were dry closings. Nobody was there from the

District of Columbia to fund the acquisition and I was coming danger-ously close to my company being homeless.

Long story short, she calls me up and she says you do not know me but I listen to your station every morning and I listen to your show. I have researched you and I have tracked you and she said, you have another closing and this will be your third and if you don't come forth with the funding you will lose the building you're trying to move your station to and I said yes.

She said well I tell you what; one of my loan officers will be there next Tuesday. We're going to fund the property acquisition for you. I said okay, what time should I meet them there and she said, you're far too busy to have to meet us there, we'll take care of it and the loan application will be in the mail. I filled the loan application out two weeks after the property was already purchased.

That is what you call a banking relationship

Bro Bedford: Yes it is. You are such a pioneer and a trailblazer. You mentioned the "Quiet Storm" and all of us listen to that but we don't know where that originated. How did you come up with the concept of doing "The Quiet Storm"?

Cathy Hughes: When I became the General Manager of Howard University Radio, WHUR, I was really excited about the opportuni-ty but I also was very much aware of what I needed to learn. So I approached Howard University and I asked them if they would allow me a six-week sabbatical to go the University of Chicago and take a summer course called Psycho-Graphic Programming. Which they said, "*yes as long as they didn't have to pay for it, I could go*". So I went at my own expense and I learned about programming a radio station to fit the listener's lifestyle.

This was before morning talk shows were popular. This was before talk radio stations were popular. What I learned in that six week class was that you can have a very successful format if you hit the right time with your audience and you service their desire.

I was in Washington, D.C and DC has always been notorious for this overpopulation of women professionals who were basically man less and dateless on Friday nights. *The Quiet Storm* started off as a Friday night experiment to entertain women who didn't have dates for the evening.

That's how I promoted it and that's why I created it and then I went from Friday night, to Saturday night, to Sunday night and the rest is history. It went from one night a week to seven nights a week. Then it went from Howard University to, in its hay day, four hundred and eight five stations used my format.

It was specifically created to entertain people who were dateless. Who were single and wanted companionship and wanting company.

Bro Bedford: Wow! I'm just blown away by the way you have pioneered certain things and again not knowing. I'm a big talk radio format fan. I just love listening to talk radio. Then to find out that in your initial stages of getting your financing, you had to overcome that obstacle or that hurdle of being a talk format or music format. Didn't you have that challenge?

Cathy Hughes: They told me that black people could not talk and that advertisers would not support black talk. But let me tell you, the interesting thing was I had a battle with the advertisers. I had a battle with the lenders. The way I ended up on the air was quite by accident. I had to host the morning show because my lending institutions told me that I was the first 24-hour news talk format from a black perspective in the United States.

My lenders told me, number one, news talk as you well know, is the most expensive of all the formats. It's a lot cheaper to just have a D.J. there spinning records. When you have a news talk format, you have to have news people. You have to have wire service. You have to have producers, researches and then you have to have hosts. So they said it's too costly, go back to doing music.

But I refused to go back to 24 hours of music because I had done research on what format was needed and wanted by the Washington, D.C. community and what they said overwhelmingly was that they wanted more news and information about themselves.

They said they could turn on any station and find out what was going on at the White House or in Chicago or Poduck, Idaho but they could not find out what was going on in Southeast, D.C., which had the highest percentage of black residents at that time.

So I knew that this was a needed format, a needed service in my community. So I started hosting it myself, but initially those first several years. My biggest battle did not come from my advertisers, or my lenders, it came from my audience itself.

My audience felt that because some black people may have left an "S" off of a verb or put on one, that they were embarrassing their entire community. I said now wait a minute; one person cracking a verb does not bring the whole black community down. My community is not that shallow and if you think that it is, then maybe you need to join somebody else's community. Okay.

I said, "*and plus we'll get the swing of this we've never been allowed to express ourselves before*". Oh I would get petitions from schoolteachers. I got a petition one day from 300 hundred black schoolteachers signed that said that my program was anti-intellectual and that I was embarrassing the black community. I said, "*you all are the embarrassment to the black community that you would be so ignorant to send this type of petition in here and try to stop black people from expressing themselves.*"

Then I had to really get a little heavy handed with them and I said if these black brothers and sisters don't know how to talk correctly on talk radio it's because you have not been doing your job, you're the teachers.

Bro Bedford: They got failed somewhere…

Cathy Hughes: Thank you. I said is this an apology. Then I read the petition on the air and read off their names. Well that was the last time that anyone ever said that black folk should not be allowed to talk in public. I just literally put a spot light on them. I said how dare you be embarrassed by your own people, you know.

Bro Bedford: Yes, yes. You know with my subscribers and this has been strange to me, not strange in fact that it cannot happen, but when I first started, of course, my initial subscribers were male. Today my subscriber base is between 70 to 75% female.

Cathy Hughes: Wow!

Bro Bedford: So my question to you, if you were to advise someone who is interested in becoming an entrepreneur, **particularly black**

women, what should be their first steps?

Cathy Hughes: The first step for any entrepreneur is to clearly define what it is that you want to do. Ideas are like noses, all of us have one and we have to really **quantify** and **qualify** our ideas because everyone has dreams and aspirations.

You have to do research, you have to read, and you have to be studied on what it is that you want to do. Unless, and I say this to a lot of women, unless you are already doing it.

So many black women are already entrepreneurs and don't realize it. Some of us have already been entrepreneurs since when we were in Jr. High school, **braiding** all of our friend's hair, okay, or **cooking** for some function, or **researching** a term paper for someone else or back in the days before computers, **typing** a term paper for somebody.

So many of us were already entrepreneurs and didn't realize it. **Babysitting, cleaning** somebody else's dorm room in college to make a few dollars, okay.

I'm like well if you're making enough money to pay your tuition in college cleaning up everybody else's dorm room, have you ever given any consideration to the possibility that maybe you should hire some other people and take over the whole campus? Ok, **open a company!** So you have to clearly define what it is that you want to do and quantify and qualify it and not just allow it to be a dream.   It's like I said, dreams are like noses, we all got dreams and ideas on something we can do.

The most important aspect of a woman going into business I think is really **identifying and forming a support group**. So often, people who love us feel the need to protect us and they sometimes over protect us and make us squeamish and afraid to be adventurous. You have to be **bold** and **adventurous** if you're a woman going into business. Even though more and more and more women are going into business, it's still a male dominated game.

So often in my case it was my mother. I can't tell you, my mother would cry and beg me to please get a government job, you're in Washington, D.C., you're smart, people like you, give up you're sleeping on the floor in a sleeping bag Cathy. People think you've lost your mind, that you had a nervous breakdown what's wrong with you. Go and get a good government job and stop trying.

My mother was not trying to stop me from being a successful entrepreneur, she was worried about me. She was scared for me. I had lost everything to try to hold on to this business and she was ready for me to throw in the towel out of love and protection. But guess what? It was also discouraging.

So I started lying to my mother. When she would call, she would say have you turned it around? I would say, oh yeah momma things are just great. But guess what? In lying to my mother about my business turning around, and doing great, I started to believe it myself. And once I started to believe it myself, guess what? It started to happen.

So I tell women so often that your husbands, your brothers, your sisters, your mothers, your daddy, your neighbors and sometimes even your financial advisors and your lawyers are the first to want to protect you.

It's so interesting, black women, we don't get a lot of help, but we get a lot of protection "**allegedly".** A lot of advice on what we should be doing which discourages us because as black women we're full of passion and emotion.

So if someone tells us we're making a mistake, most of us unless we're just knuckle heads, most of us will stop and analyze it. Am I really acting crazy? I am sleeping in a sleeping bag, like my momma said and cooking on a hot plate. Maybe I am not really realizing. Okay.

So you have to put on blinders. You have to be myopic. You have to keep your eye on the prize. You cannot sometimes share with people. You have to lie. When people say, how is it going? They may be getting ready to foreclose on your underwear, but you got to say, I can't tell you today was just fabulous.

Both Laugh

Bro Bedford: The best day I've had

36

Cathy Hughes: The best day I've had since I've been in business. Like I said, if you say it enough, the first person that you're going to convince is yourself because who's hearing it more than anybody else, you.

Bro. Bedford: Right.

Cathy Hughes: Your attitude really does determine your altitude. Your attitude determines your altitude. But like I said, with women we normally can't get a lot a financial or other help. Sometimes you don't need the finances; you just need someone to give you a helping hand. But Lord have mercy, do people give us advice under the guise of I'm just trying to protect you. I'm just trying to look out for you. Well if you're trying to look out for me, loan me that $10K I need to make payroll.

Both Laugh

Okay. I don't need you discouraging me. It's funny because people want to be politically correct. They don't say to you point blank that you shouldn't be doing this. They say things like; well do you think it's really worth it? Do you think that you're maybe sacrificing too much? What about you? What about your own personal life?

I'm trying to build a business right now; **my business is my personal life.**

So I tell women, don't get discouraged and try to find somebody in a comparable situation, if not maybe the same situation but a comparable situation.

People are amazed because entrepreneurs call me frequently and their like, you took my call. I'm like yeah because I can't tell you how lonely it was for me when no one would take my call.

I say it might take me a few weeks and sometimes, if I get back logged maybe a couple months. I've called people back and they're like I forgot I called you Ms. Hughes. I say, I will return your call; you've just got to be patient because sometimes it's just a word of encouragement that we need to get over the hump.

Bro Bedford: Wow that's beautiful. I saw you on the Tavis Smiley's *State of the Black Union* the other day. I listened and watched just as I just heard you speak now, when I listen to you, when I see you, I hear a woman with **passion** and **drive.** Will you expound on your passion and what drives you?

Cathy Hughes: God. I have a firm belief that God has used me as an instrument to be a voice for my people and as a vehicle for the upliftment and betterment for my people. I have twenty five hundred employees, of that about twenty-two hundred are of African descent and of that about 44% are women.

That's not me. That's not a result of anything special about me. That's a classic example of God using an ordinary woman to do extraordinary things for other individuals.

My motivation, my passion, my commitment, my determination is all predicated on this deep, deep, deep, deep commitment and desire to leave my community just a little bit better when I close my eyes for the final time, then it was when I opened my eyes for the first time.

I love my people. I love my community and I feel that it is an obligation that I have been charged with and a responsibility that I welcome to help as many black folks as I possibly can.

I believe in the old adage *"that a rising tide lifts all boats"*. So I feel that God has allowed my boat to rise with the tides, so that I can bring some other boats up with me.

Bro. Bedford: That's beautiful. I know you have to go but I have one last question if you don't mind.

Cathy Hughes: No go right ahead.

Bro Bedford: Yes. We just talked about your passion and your drive and in fact just many traits and characteristics that you have that just flow out of you. But what trait or characteristic do you think a person must have, if they are to achieve success as an entrepreneur?

Cathy Hughes: **Integrity.** Your word must be your bond. Again if I could just share with you a little bit, I'm the Time Warner Endowed Chair for the Howard University School of Communications. I tell my class frequently that integrity; **your word has to be your bond**. You know the Japanese don't use lawyers; their word is their bond. They have a thriving economy based on the fact that you have to be an honorable human being.

I tell my classes that one of the biggest mistakes that entrepreneurs make is that they run from the people that they owe money to, their creditors. When they know that they can't make the payment, and we do this so much in our personal lives to. I say to them what I'm getting ready to share with you will work in your personal life as well as in your business life.

When you owe someone something, you have given them your word that you're going to pay them back. So when you're not able to, you owe them an explanation or at bare minimum a notification that you're not going to be able to live up to your word.

So I tell them, I use this strategy and it's why I was never foreclosed on. When I couldn't make my payments, no creditor had to call me because I was calling them saying listen, Bro. Bedford, I am so sorry. I know I owe you a $1000, I don't have your $1,000 dollars next Tuesday when it's due, but I do have $200 dollars and I'm going to send you that $200 and I'm going to make good on that $800 dollars that I owe you as soon as I possibly can.

No I can't tell you exactly when that day is going to be, but I'm going to send you $25, $50 or $100 dollars the next minute I get my hands on it so that I can retire this debt as soon as possible. But I want you to know that I acknowledge that I owe you this $1000 dollars and Bro. Bedford, my word is my bond, you will be paid.

Every single solitary one of my creditors got some type of payment from me. It was so interesting because oftentimes I would get a letter back saying, "hey your payment is so small that it's not worth us processing it and obviously you need it more than us, here's your check back."

Both Laugh

Okay, I was like thank you Lord, it worked I needed that check back, okay.

I tell people, it's the same with your personal life. I can't tell you over the years as I was growing in my business as well as my personal life, I'd be at one of my friend's house and the phone would ring and it would be a bill collector and they'd say, "tell them I'm not here, tell them I'm not home." I'd be like no you need to say that you are here and that you don't have their money. Okay. It makes a big difference.

Integrity I think is the most important trait because if you require that of yourself, the universal order of things, the God given force that controls the whole universe that keeps the Sun up in the sky and keeps the planet Earth from bumping into other planets. There is a universal God force at work, 24/7 and if you're a person of integrity, then that's what will be drawn to you. If you try to be slick and avoid the people that you owe money to or cut corners or not live up to your word, well guess what that's what you're going to attract.

So in my opinion, integrity is the most important characteristic to be a successful entrepreneur.

Bro Bedford: Ms. Hughes, I cannot explain and words do not describe that this has been a highlight for my career thus far.

Cathy Hughes: Oh aren't you a kind person, thank you.

Bro Bedford: No, I really appreciate you. I mean I've heard numerous great things about you. But to personally get an opportunity to speak to you and feel your spirit has done wonders for my soul. Thank you very much for your time.
Cathy Hughes: Thank you. God bless you and I pray that in the not too distant future you will have **one million subscribers** to your services.

Bro. Bedford: Thank you very much.

Cathy Hughes: Thank you so much for the honor of being included.

Bro Bedford: Thank you.

Cathy Hughes: Bye-Bye

www.ingramcontent.com/pod-product-compliance
Lightning Source LLC
Chambersburg PA
CBHW071646170526
45166CB00003B/1457